POLICE CARS

by Keli Sipperley

PEBBLE
a capstone imprint

Pebble Emerge is published by Pebble, an imprint of Capstone.
1710 Roe Crest Drive
North Mankato, Minnesota 56003
www.capstonepub.com

Library of Congress Cataloging-in-Publication Data
Names: Sipperley, Keli, author.
Title: Police cars / by Keli Sipperley.
Description: North Mankato, Minnesota : Pebble, [2022] | Series:
Wild about wheels | Includes bibliographical references and index. |
Audience: Ages 6–8. | Audience: Grades 2–3. | Summary: "Lights flash and
sirens sound! A police car is on its way! Police cars keep our roads and
neighborhoods safe. Police cars are fast and carry equipment for
fighting crime. Young readers will find out about police cars, their
main parts, and how these important vehicles are used"—Provided by
publisher.
Identifiers: LCCN 2020025526 (print) | LCCN 2020025527 (ebook) | ISBN 9781977132369
(library binding) | ISBN 9781977133304 (paperback) | ISBN 9781977154750 (ebook pdf)
Subjects: LCSH: Police vehicles—Juvenile literature.
Classification: LCC HV7936.V4 S56 2021 (print) | LCC HV7936.V4 (ebook) |
DDC 363.2028/4—dc23
LC record available at https://lccn.loc.gov/2020025526
LC ebook record available at https://lccn.loc.gov/2020025527

Image Credits
Alamy: Todd Bannor, 11; Capstone Studio: Karon Dubke, 7, 10, 16, 17, 21 (art supplies); Getty Images: Peter Macdiarmid, 13; iStockphoto: Evgen Prozhyrko, 6; Shutterstock: Brad Sauter, 9, Jne Valokuvaus, 8, Leonard Zhukovsky, 18–19, Marek Piotrowski (background), throughout, meunierd, 12, 14, Photo Spirit, cover, back cover, Red Orange, 21 (drawing), Schmidt_Alex, 15, stockelements, 5

Editorial Credits
Editor: Amy McDonald Maranville; Designer: Cynthia Della-Rovere; Media Researcher: Eric Gohl;
Production Specialist: Katy LaVigne

Printed and bound in China.   004205

Table of Contents

Words in **bold** are in the glossary.

What Police Cars Do

Something is wrong. Help is needed. An officer hops into a police car. Zoom! Help is on the way! Lights flash. A siren sounds. They tell people there is an **emergency**.

Police officers keep communities safe. Every day, police cars help officers do their jobs.

LOOK INSIDE

A police car is like an office on wheels. It carries the tools officers need. A computer is near the driver. The police car also has a control box inside. It has switches for the lights and siren. A two-way radio lets officers talk to one another.

Police officers make sure people follow the law. A **radar device** in the police car checks a driver's speed. Sometimes people drive too fast. The officer might make a traffic stop.

radar

camera

Many police cars have dashboard cameras. The camera records what happens during the stop. People can look at the recording later to see what happened.

Every second is important in an emergency. Police cars need speed! A police car has a big **engine** under the hood. The engine powers the police car.

A key starts the engine. Most car engines turn off when the key is taken out. Some police car engines can stay on after the key is removed. This keeps the engine warm so the car can take off quickly after a stop.

Look Outside

Police officers face dangers every day. Police cars can help protect them. The doors and windows are made with bulletproof materials. This helps keep officers safe.

Flooded streets. High speeds. Quick turns. Police car tires have extra **traction** to make driving safer.

Sometimes heavy objects block roads. Police cars have push bumpers on the front. These are used to move broken cars and other large items out of the way.

The light bar on top of a police car can flash in different patterns. Sometimes they flash just one color. Other times they flash two or more.

Every police department is different, depending on what the town needs. Their cars are different too! They are painted different colors. They have the name of the department on the sides and back. Some police cars have town **symbols** too. What do police cars look like where you live?

symbol

POLICE CAR DIAGRAM

tire

light bar

bulletproof windshield

push bumper

symbol

Design a Police Car

Police cars are built for safety and speed. Imagine you are designing a police car. It can have anything you want! What makes it fast? Does it have a special symbol on the sides?

Draw a picture of the outside of your police car. Then draw a picture of the inside.

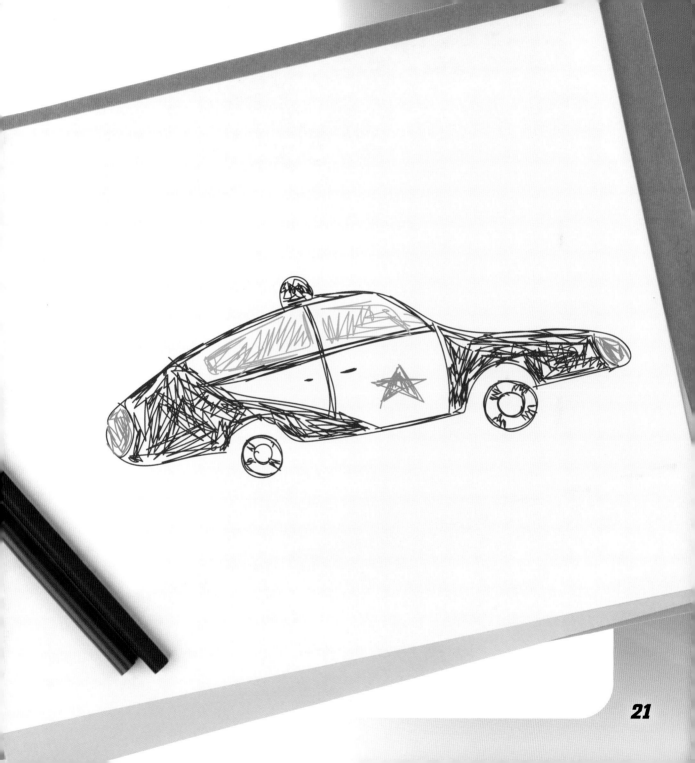

Glossary

emergency (i-MUR-juhn-see)—a sudden, dangerous situation that requires immediate action

engine (EN-juhn)—a machine that uses fuel to power a vehicle

radar device (RAY-dahr di-VISE)—a piece of equipment that measures the speed of vehicles

symbol (SIM-buhl)—a design that stands for or represents something else

traction (TRAK-shuh)—the force that keeps a moving object from slipping on a surface

Read More

Best, B.J. *Police Cars*. New York: Cavendish Square Publishing, 2018.

Kelly, Erin Suzanne. *Rescue Vehicles*. New York: Children's Press, 2021.

Schuh, Mari C. *Rescue Vehicles*. North Mankato, MN: Pebble, a Capstone imprint, 2019.

Internet Sites

Child Fun: Police Activities
www.childfun.com/themes/people/police/

Kiddle: Police Car Facts for Kids
kids.kiddle.co/Police_car

Safe Kid Games: Driving Games
www.safekidgames.com/driving-games/

Index